To Marsha
From Cerie
Jan

Marsha

Happy Holidays

To my dear dear

friend! Love
Jan

KEEPERS *of the* DREAM

Patricia Wyatt

Pomegranate Artbooks · San Francisco

Published by Pomegranate Artbooks
Box 6099, Rohnert Park, California 94927

Pomegranate Europe Ltd.
Fullbridge House, Fullbridge
Maldon, Essex CM9 7LE, England

Library of Congress Cataloging-in-Publication Data

Wyatt, Patricia.
    Keepers of the dream/Patricia Wyatt.—1st ed.
        p.   cm.
    ISBN 0-87654-477-4
    1. Wyatt, Patricia—Themes, motives. 2. Indian women—Pictorial works.
    3. Indians—Religion and mythology—Pictorial works.
    I. Title
    ND237.W92A4   1995
    759.13—dc20   95-30719
                                        CIP
Pomegranate Catalog No. A805

Designed by John Malmquist Design

Printed in Korea
00 99 98 97 96 95   6 5 4 3 2 1

First Edition

CONTENTS

The land, the people, the animals, and their stories have inspired me to create the paintings in this book. The land is filled with the myths of the ancient people and their kindred animal spirits. They live between the earth and the sky, they listen to the voice of the wind, they live their dreams, they answer to Mother Earth, they sing the song of the spirit, and they have ultimate faith in the Great Mystery.

The Grandmothers say eagles are spirit people
who live in a special
home in the sky
they say in winter and spring the
eagles come to earth through a hole in the sky to dance, to sing
to build their nests, to lay their
eggs, to hatch their young and to
leave their dreams among the cliffs
of the mountains and high mesas

I dedicate these paintings to breaking the boundaries that separate us, to all the people who share their dreams and myths with each other, and to my son, Theo, and the woman he loves.

—Patricia Wyatt
Santa Fe, New Mexico, 1995

Introduction

Patricia Wyatt lives in the American Southwest under a vault of blue in a land of sage and clay. The colors of the landscape merge in her palette; the stories of the people, ancient tales, pulse in her hands.

Wyatt's *Medicine Women* (Pomegranate Artbooks, 1993) walk with a singular grace and beauty. In *Keepers of the Dream,* ancient peoples have invited her to a new artistic threshold, a place where their voices rise powerfully from within the storytelling traditions of North and South American cultures. Their myths—Maya and Aztec, Lakota, Acoma, Apache—have brought Wyatt's work to a point of great liberation.

Each painting in *Keepers of the Dream* is a response to a particular story. The images testify to the power of myth to heal, inform, and unite. The myths, experienced through strong archetypes, speak to the need for power, vision, responsibility, community, beauty, and love in our daily walk. They break the boundaries between people, bringing them together in the peace of ancient wisdom. Though grounded in ancient rituals, the stories and images frame our contemporary experience, rekindling our spirits and restoring our sense of wonder in the world.

Wyatt's perception of myths as paintings challenges our increasing bias toward language. "Painting is not an unusual way to pass on myth or story," she says. "In presenting the viewer with a visual myth, the painting carries on an ancient artistic tradition."

In addition to presenting myths from various North and South American cultures, I have taken this opportunity to explore my own personal mythology. I hope those of you who take pleasure in these myths will take the time to develop your own myths in words, song, dance, or painting, as I believe this mythology helps us comprehend our individual lives.

The teachings in Keepers of the Dream *heal by guiding us through our most challenging passages. In our hectic lives, we often lose sight of the path. Like a loop in a weaving, myth is the way out and the way back in. These stories and paintings offer each of us a quiet moment in which to consider the needs of our souls. May these paintings and stories inspire you to integrity. May you arise from your time with this book as if you had spent a night at the storyteller's hearth, listening to the rise and fall of Grandmother's voice murmuring from the shadows. May it call you to beauty.*

—Patricia Wyatt

The White Buffalo Woman

LONG AGO one summer the seven sacred council fires of the Lakota Oyate camped together, but there was no game to be found for food. The chief of the Itazipcho band, Standing Hollow Horn, sent two of his men to hunt. While climbing a high hill they saw a figure floating toward them, and they knew that this was a *wakan,* or holy person.

The figure was that of an extraordinarily beautiful young woman with two red dots on her cheeks; she wore a shining white buckskin. The *wakan* woman was Ptosan-Wi, White Buffalo Woman. She carried a large bundle and a sage leaf fan. All but one strand of her blue-black hair was loose; that strand was tied up with buffalo fur. Her dark, luminous eyes held great power.

Both men stared at the woman. One desired her, and tried to touch her. He was immediately struck with lightning and burned to a small pile of bones. White Buffalo Woman told the remaining hunter to tell his people to build a medicine lodge to prepare for her arrival in the camp. She said, "I am bringing something holy to your nation."

The lodge was built, and after four days, the people saw her approaching. Chief Standing Hollow Horn invited White Buffalo Woman to enter the lodge, and she circled the interior sunwise and then instructed the people to build a sacred earth altar. She circled the lodge once more, stopping before the chief to open her bundle. It was the *chanunpa,* the sacred pipe.

Grasping the stem with her right hand and the bowl with her left, she lit the pipe and showed the people how to hold it from that time forward. She explained that this eternal fire was to be passed to all generations and that the rising smoke was the breath of great Grandfather Mystery.

She taught the people how to pray with the holy pipe and explained how their bodies and the pipe, held stem to the sky, formed a link between what was sacred below and above, making all creation one family: the earth, sky, every living thing, the two-legged and four-legged, the winged ones, the trees, and the grasses. The stone bowl, she said, represented both the buffalo and the red man, and the buffalo represented the universe and the four directions. Finally she explained that the seven circles engraved in the bowl stand for the seven sacred ceremonies practiced with the pipe and the seven sacred campfires of the Lakota nation.

Silhouetted against the sun, White Buffalo Woman walked away from the Lakota people, stopping four times to roll on the ground. She turned into a black buffalo the first time, then a brown one, then a red one, and finally she became the sacred white female buffalo calf. After she disappeared, great herds of buffalo arrived, providing meat, skin, and bones for the Lakotas' food, clothing, shelter, and tools.

A tale of the LAKOTA

White Buffalo Calf Woman, 1994
Mixed media on paper, 50 x 40 in.

How the First Vine Grew

THE WIND GOD, EHECATL, was traveling in his usual ways when he saw and fell in love with a beautiful girl called Mayahuel, who was living in the home of the gods. She was under the guardianship of an old woman called Tzitzimil. One night when all were asleep in the home of the gods, Ehecatl came as a gentle breeze. He softly awakened Mayahuel and carried her away without waking her guardian.

By the time they arrived back on the Earth the love between Ehecatl and Hayahuel had become a whirlwind. As their feet touched the ground they spun together, forming a great tall tree with two strong branches. Ehecatl's branch grew shining green leaves, and Mayahuel's branch grew fragrant white blossoms.

In the meantime, the guardian Tzitzimil awoke to find Mayahuel gone. In fury she set out to find and punish the lovers.

Circling the earth, she spied the wondrous tree, immediately recognizing Mayahuel in the flowering branch. She called on the god of lightning to strike the tree and sever Mayahuel from her lover. She then tore the branch into a thousand pieces and scattered them far and wide.

The grieving Ehecatl resumed his normal self. Mourning the loss of his love, he gathered the scattered fragments and tenderly buried them. As soon as he had covered the last one with a handful of earth, a small green shoot appeared. This is how the first vine came to be, from which the people have learned to make wine, which they love much as Ehecatl loved Mayahuel.

A tale of the AZTEC

Touched by Hummingbird, 1994
Mixed media on paper, 50 x 40 in.

The Woman Who Married a Frog

THE CHIEF had a young daughter who was as proud as she was beautiful. She refused all suitors because she felt they were not good enough. One day she and her sister went for a walk beside a large lake near their village. A great many frogs were sunning themselves on a mud bank in the middle of the lake. The proud maiden said to her sister, "How ugly those creatures are." Seeing a very large frog near her feet on the shore, she picked him up, saying, "You certainly are an ugly fellow. I'll bet even another frog would not want to marry you!" Then she threw the frog roughly back into the lake.

That night, while her family was asleep, the proud maiden decided to walk in the moonlight. As she stepped outside the lodge she saw a handsome young man dressed in beautiful garments decorated with fine green beads. "I've come to marry you," the young man said. "Come with me to my father's house." The young woman had never seen such a handsome man before, and she very much wanted to be his wife, and so she followed him as he walked toward the lake. At the edge of the lake he continued to walk, and soon they both disappeared under the water.

The next day her family members searched everywhere for her. Finally they saw the tracks leading to the water and decided that she must have drowned. They cut their hair and blackened their faces and mourned their loss.

One day, about a year after the maiden had disappeared, the younger daughter was walking near the lake and thought she saw her sister on the mud bank in the middle of the lake. She ran to her parents, saying, "Come quickly, I have seen my sister. She has been taken by the frogs because she insulted them."

The chief knew what he must do. He made offering to the frog people, asking them to forgive his daughter. He placed dishes of food and fine skins on the bank and he saw his daughter and the frog people come and take the gifts, but his daughter did not return to her family. At last he gathered all the people, asking their help, for he had a plan to get his daughter back. "We will dig a trench and drain the water of the lake so that we can rescue my daughter," he told the people.

The people worked hard, and soon the water began to drain away. The frog people tried to fill the trench, but they could not keep the water from draining out of the lake. The frogs tried to drive the people away, but the people gently picked up the frogs and set them back in the lake. At last, just as the frog village was almost destroyed, the chief of the frogs called his people together, saying, "We are not strong enough to fight these humans. I will tell my son that he must give up his wife in order to save our people." They took the young woman to the place where the people were digging the trench, and her mother and father saw her and pulled her out.

Lovers of the Lake (detail), 1995
Mixed media on paper, 14 x 40 in.

She was covered with mud and smelled like a frog. One huge frog leaped out of the water after her. It was her husband, the frog chief's son. The young woman's sister lifted the frog with great respect and gently put him back in the lake. Then they took the young woman home.

For a long time the once proud daughter could only speak as frogs do, saying, "Huh, huh, huh!" After a while she learned to speak like a human again, and she told the people, "The frogs know our language, so we must not speak badly about them." From that day on, the people showed great respect to the frogs. They learned the songs that the woman brought back from the frog people, and they used the frog as an emblem so they would never forget what had happened to the young woman who was too proud. To this day, when people hear the frogs singing in the lake they know that the frogs are telling their children this story, too.

A tale of the TLINGIT

Morning Star and Evening Star

OVER ALL is Terawahat, the One Above, changeless and supreme. From Terawahat come all things; Terawahat made the heavens and the stars.

Long ago there dwelt in the west White Star Woman, who is the Evening Star. Until she was found and overcome there could be no creation on the Earth. It was decided that Great Star of Morning was to find White Star Woman so that creation could begin at last.

Morning Star called his brother and asked him for help with this great task, for he needed someone to carry his sacred medicine bundle. As they journeyed, White Star Woman moved and came near, drawing Morning Star to her. (For men may see how the Evening Star moves nightly. One night she is low in the heavens and another night she is high in the heavens. Even so, she moved and drew Morning Star.) Morning Star was joyful, but then he saw that White Star Woman had placed in his path hard things to hinder his approach, even as she rose and beckoned him, looking upon his face. He started toward her, but the Earth opened and great waters swept down. In the waters was a great serpent, his mouth open wide, ready to devour. Morning Star called to his brother. Then from his medicine bag he took a ball of fire, which he threw into the serpent's huge mouth. White Star Woman put ten more hardships in his way, but he overcame them all and soon was at the door of her lodge. He found that she was guarded by the powerful beasts of the four directions in the form of great stars.

Morning Star proclaimed that he had conquered and fulfilled the hardships placed before him and commanded that the guardians obey him, saying, "Black Star stand in the northeast, whence cometh the night; you are Autumn. Yellow Star stand in the northwest, where the golden sun sets; you are Spring. White Star stand in the south, facing north, whence cometh the snow; you are Winter. Red Star you shall stand in the southeast; you are Summer."

After Morning Star provided water in the form of rain to keep Evening Star's gardens forever green, he and White Star Woman lay together. In celebration they created the Sun to provide heat and light for the Earth. From the union of Morning Star and Evening Star came a maiden who married the son of the Moon, and together they peopled the Earth.

A tale of the SKIDI PAWNEE

Peacemaker, 1994
Mixed media on paper, 40 x 60 in.

The Old Woman Who Lived with Wolves

THE SIOUX were people who moved from one place to another within their borders. Long ago while the entire village was moving, a young woman named Matpiyawin romped along playing with her beloved dog. One evening during this journey she noticed that her dog was missing. She thought it might have been coaxed away by a wolf pack, which was not uncommon. After thinking the situation over, she decided to go back the way she had come to look for the dog.

While she was traveling back, it began to snow and she sought shelter in a cave. She fell asleep in the cave and had a wonderful vision about wolves who talked to her, saying that she should trust them and that they would not let her suffer from cold or hunger. When she awoke, wolves were sitting alongside her in the cave. She remained with them for several days while a blizzard raged outside the cave. They supplied her with food and kept her warm with their shaggy coats. When the weather cleared, she needed to leave the cave. She thanked the wolves for their kindness and asked what she could do to repay them. They asked that she bring food to the top of the hill for them when the long winter months came and food became scarce. She gladly promised to do this.

Soon after she left, the young woman came to the camp of her people. They were happy to see her; they had thought that she had been taken by an enemy tribe and that they might never see her again. She pointed to the top of the hill where her wolf companions were and explained that she had been lost and had been saved by these wolves.

Ever after, when winter came Matpiyawin took meat to these wolves. She never forgot their language, and in winter they could be heard calling to her. They would warn the tribe of bad weather or of an enemy passing close by, or just let her know that they were watching out for her.

And so she came to be known as Old Woman Who Lived with Wolves.

A tale of the SIOUX

Wolf Loyalty Leads to Courage, 1994
Mixed media on canvas, 50 x 70 in.

The Marriage of the Sun and the Moon

THERE WAS ONCE a man who lived in the woods with his beautiful daughter. Each day, as the daughter sat at her loom weaving, a young and handsome hunter would pass their home with a freshly killed deer slung over his shoulders.

One day, the girl was washing maize so that it could be cooked. When she had finished, she took the water outside the hut and poured it out on the path in front of her home. The water made the path very slippery, and when the hunter, bearing the day's kill, passed by, he fell and dropped the deer. When the deer hit the ground, it became obvious that this was not fresh meat at all, but in fact was a skin filled with red-hot embers and ashes. The hot ashes spilled out, crackling and smoking between the hunter and the girl. The hunter was not an ordinary man, but the Sun himself. Having been found out, the Sun turned himself into a hummingbird and flew away as fast as he could.

The Sun Man remembered the girl and decided to see her again as the hummingbird. He returned to the garden near her hut and fed on the flowers that grew there. The girl spotted the hummingbird fluttering in the trees and asked her father to bring it to her. The man shot the bird with his sling and brought the stunned bird to his daughter.

The girl took the bird gently into her hands and kept him safe and warm all day. At night her father locked her into the safest and warmest part of the hut; she took the hummingbird with her.

In the warm room, the hummingbird revived and saw the girl sleeping by the fire. The Sun returned to his human shape and woke the girl. She was very happy to see the young hunter.

"Come with me into the woods," said the hunter.

"I would like to, but we are locked in the hut by my father," said the girl.

"We can escape still, for I can change our shapes."

"But he has a magic lens with which he can see us wherever we go," said the girl.

"Do not worry, I can take care of that," said the hunter. And with that, they were transformed and escaped through the keyhole. In a short time they were far from the girl's hut.

When the girl's father awoke the following morning, he discovered that his daughter was missing. "That was no ordinary hummingbird," he said to himself. "Whatever it was, it must have bewitched her." The man went for his magic lens to look for the girl, but when he put it to his eye he found it full of hot chili powder, which burned his eye so that he could not see anything at all.

Angry and in pain, the man called out to the volcano to stop the girl and the hunter. A shower of fire and sparks suddenly shot out of the volcano and flew toward the couple. Just as the rain of fire approached the pair, the Sun Man spotted a tortoise. "Please, friend tortoise, let us hide in your shell," pleaded the hunter. The tortoise could not see how all three of them could fit in his already small shell.

Celestial Bodies (detail), 1995
Mixed media on paper, 50 x 30 in.

The hunter, however, was a shape changer and quickly shrank down small enough to slip in beside the tortoise. Just as the hunter was saying the words that would allow the girl to join him in the safety of the shell, the rain of fire engulfed her and she was scattered into a thousand pieces.

The rain of fire was followed by a flood, which washed the girl into a large lake. The Sun Man ordered everyone to collect the pieces and place them in water in hundreds of skins, pots, and containers of every kind. When all the containers were full, he took them to an innkeeper and told him he would return for them in two weeks. After a few days the innkeeper noticed the containers were moving.

The hunter returned as he had promised, and the innkeeper immediately asked what was in the containers. "All is well," said the young man. "Look inside and see." Inside all the bottles, pots, and sacks were little animals. However, in one, there was a tiny figure of the girl. When she saw the hunter, she waved and smiled: the girl had been brought back to life.

The hunter soon returned her to normal size using his powerful magic. The young man resumed his duties as the Sun, and the girl, who soon became his wife, turned into the Moon.

A tale of the MAYA

The Bear and His Wife

QUISS-AN-KWEEDASS AND KIND-A-WUSS had been in love with each other since childhood. By their tribe's social law, they knew that they could never live as husband and wife because both were of one crest, the Raven.

When it came time to marry, their parents reminded them that they had to choose others outside their crest. The parents tried to keep them apart, but they failed. Confined to their separate homes, the lovers escaped.

They ran to the woods, where they lived until the lengthening nights and stormy days of winter. Quiss-An-Kweedass resolved to visit his family while Kind-A-Wuss remained in the forest. He promised to return for her in four days. But he was held prisoner by his family. Finally, Quiss-An-Kweedass was able to return to the place where he had left Kind-A-Wuss, but she was not to be found. Search parties were sent out to look for her, but months turned into years and she was not found.

Quiss-An-Kweedass never forgot his beloved. Years later he set out with the help of a medicine man to search for Kind-A-Wuss. This time it did not take long to find her. Kind-A-Wuss had fallen in love with a bear while waiting for Quiss-An-Kweedass to return. Her bear husband had done everything he could to make her happy and comfortable. He did everything in his power to please her. During their time together, they had two sons, and he wrote a song for her declaring his love and kind feelings for her.

Eventually Kind-A-Wuss returned to her people. The song written for her by her bear husband became the tribe's "Song of the Bear." Whoever could sing it would have the everlasting friendship of all bears.

A tale of the HAIDAS

Bear Love, 1994
Mixed media on paper,
50 x 40 in.

The Star Woman

A MAN had a beautiful wife who became sick and died. After her death, feeling sad, he would go out into the village plaza at night and lie down on a leaf of the *bacaba* palm. One night a brilliant star that he had been watching suddenly left the sky and reappeared next to him. Asking him to move over a little so they could lie together on the leaf, the star began to talk. They talked all night, and at dawn she returned to the heavens. This happened for five nights. On the fifth night the Star Woman agreed to marry the man. He put her into a large gourd, which he hung up in his house. After that he opened the gourd whenever he wished, and they would converse.

One day when the man was not at home, his sister became suspicious. She looked in the gourd and saw the Star Woman. When her brother returned, she told him that he must no longer hide a woman in his room, but must take her as his wife. So the Star Woman became his wife. She asked for a garden plot of her own, but her husband did not understand, as the people then ate only rotten wood, leaves, and wild coconuts.

By way of explanation, the Star Woman threw a long cotton thread up into the sky and climbed up, soon returning with yams and potatoes. The man refused to eat these foods for he was afraid they would make him sick. The Star Woman held his head and forced him to eat. He liked the food and told all the others to eat as well. He helped the Star Woman with the garden plot, and she went to the sky many times and brought the people corn, beans, rice, and peanuts, which the people plant until this day. She also taught the people to make mats, bags, and other things of straw.

The people learned many things from the Star Woman, but her husband ran off with another woman and she returned to the sky. If her husband had been faithful to her, she would have continued to bring gifts to the people of the Earth. Because of an unfaithful husband, the people do not have all the good things that exist in the heavens.

A tale of the APINAYE

Her Heart Makes These Buds Bloom, 1994
Mixed media on paper, 40 x 48 in.

Tolowim Woman and Butterfly Man

IT WAS A BEAUTIFUL SPRING. It was time for spearing salmon and hunting deer. Tolowim Woman was alone, restless and lonely. Her husband was away with the other men hunting and fishing, and this is a time when men must not be with their wives. Tolowim Woman was a good wife, but she, too, felt the spring, and she had grown weary of women's voices. Early one morning she put on her basket hat, left her house, and turned away from the river and the village and began a walk into the green hills. It was a lovely morning.

By midday the sun was quite hot, and Tolowim Woman found some shade in which to rest under a manzanita bush. She slept for a while, awakening to a gentle brushing on her cheek. Opening her eyes, she beheld the most beautiful butterfly she had ever seen. Laughing, Tolowim Woman tried to touch the butterfly when it landed on a branch above her, but it fluttered away. She took her seed basket hat and attempted to capture it, but again it fluttered just out of reach. She decided that she must have this beautiful creature, and so she got up and began to follow the butterfly.

All through the afternoon it led her on, deeper into the hills and away from her home. Soon her buckskin skirt was dirty and torn, her basket hat lost, and her shell necklace broken and scattered, but she cared not and continued to follow the splendid butterfly.

As the sun sank low, the butterfly appeared to turn toward her. It settled on the earth at her feet. Suddenly in the dusky light Tolowim Woman saw a handsome, graceful man, naked save for the butterfly girdle around his slim waist. His hair was long and was held back in a red and black headband.

Together they passed the night, and in the morning Butterfly Man said, "I am going to my home. Do you wish to come with me?"

"Oh, yes," replied Tolowim Woman.

"It will take only one more day, but it is a dangerous and difficult journey, for we must cross the Valley of the Butterflies, and they will surely try to take you from me. Will you do as I say so that I may safely lead you through this danger?"

Tolowim Woman promised to do as he told her. Then he instructed her, "Follow closely; step where I step. Hold tight to my girdle; do not let go even for a moment. Do not look at any other butterfly until we are safely out of the valley. Obey me now and you will be safe forever. If you let go of my girdle even for a moment, I cannot protect you."

They began the hard journey, going fast and straight. As they entered the Valley of the Butterflies, the air seemed entirely filled with butterflies. The butterflies beat their wings against the pair's arms and legs, fluttered in their faces and caught in their hair. Tolowim Woman held fast to Butterfly Man's girdle with downcast eyes, lest she look at another butterfly. Suddenly a huge all-black butterfly hovered before her, grazing her breasts and moving into her line of vision. She closed her eyes for a moment so that she wouldn't look at him, and he settled for a

Changing Woman, 1995
Mixed media on paper,
48 x 36 in.

brief moment on her lips. Tolowim Woman was so startled that she opened her eyes and gazed at this huge butterfly, drinking in his beauty. As he began to move away from her she took one hand from Butterfly Man's girdle to reach for this black beauty. And he was gone. At once a hundred thousand butterflies danced before her, white, yellow, black, purple, gold, green, orange. She reached for them all but could not catch them.

Butterfly Man never looked back. For a while she could see him running through this sea of fluttering beauty, and then he was gone. She ran after one and then another, always reaching, always missing. Disheveled, obsessed, her hair unbraided, her skirt just rags, her moccasins in shreds, she continued her hopeless chase until her heart stopped beating.

A tale of the MAIDU

Creation of the Animal People

EARTH was once a human being. The Old One said Earth was made out of a woman, and that she would be the mother of all people.

It is said that Earth is alive, that her flesh is the soil, that her bones are the rocks, that her breath is the wind, that grass and trees are her hair, and that we live on her and that we have an earthquake when she moves.

After the Old One turned woman into Earth, he then gathered some of her flesh and rolled it into balls as people do with clay or mud. He made the first group of these balls into the ancient beings of the early world. The ancients were people as well as animals. Some looked like humans, while some walked on all fours. Some could fly, and some could swim like fish. All the ancients could speak.

The Old One made people and animals into male and female so that they could multiply—bears, birds, insects, mountain lions, from the biggest to the smallest creatures.

Thus all living things come from the Mother Earth.

A tale of the OKANOGAN

Mother Earth's Relations, 1995
Mixed media on canvas, 50 x 70 in.

The End of the World

AT A PLACE where the prairie and the badlands meet there is a well-hidden cave. In it lives a woman so old that her face looks like a shriveled-up walnut. She is dressed in rawhide, the way people dressed long, long ago. She has been sitting there for a thousand years or more, working on a blanket strip made of dyed porcupine quills, the way the ancestors always did. Her teeth are worn flat, worn down to stumps from flattening so many porcupine quills.

Resting beside her is Shunka Sapa, a huge black dog. He licks his paws and watches her. His eyes never wander from the old woman.

A few steps from where they sit a warm fire is kept going. The woman lit this fire a thousand or more years ago, and she has kept it burning ever since. Over the fire hangs a big earthen pot, the kind the people have always made from the clay of Mother Earth. Inside the pot *wojapi* is boiling and bubbling. *Wojapi* is berry soup, good, sweet, and red. The soup has been boiling in the pot for as long as the fire has been burning.

Every now and then the old woman gets up to stir the *wojapi* in the pot. She is so old and feeble that it takes her a while to get up and hobble over to the fire. The moment her back is turned, the huge dog starts pulling the porcupine quills out of her blanket strip. In this way she never makes any progress and her quill work remains forever unfinished. The Sioux people say that if the old woman ever finishes her blanket strip, at that moment, as she threads the last porcupine quill and completes the design, the world will come to an end.

A tale of the WHITE RIVER SIOUX

Keepers of the World's Life Force, 1995
Mixed media on paper, 30 x 40 in.

How Men and Women Got Together

OLD MAN made the world and everything on it. He did it very well except that he put men and women in separate places. And so they lived for a long time. They did everything the same way. They herded buffalo over steep cliffs and butchered them for meat, which was their only food. After some time the men learned to make bows and arrows for hunting and the women learned to tan hides and make beautiful tipis and clothing that they decorated with porcupine quills.

One day Old Man sat thinking about his creations and he thought he had made a bad mistake putting men and women in separate places, for there was no pleasure in that and no children. He thought a lot about this and decided that he would bring them together and put much pleasure in this so that men and women would want to mate.

"I will set an example," he said. Traveling to where the women were living, he hid behind some trees, watching. "What a good life these women have," he thought. "They have fine tipis of hides and fine clothes with beautiful decorations. The men live in brush shelters and have only rawhide loincloths. I really made a big mistake putting women so far away. They could live with us and make these fine things for us as well."

Old Man went back to the men's camp and told them about all the wonders he had seen. The men said, "Let us go over there and get together with these different human beings." Old Man told them that he was planning to create something else, something very pleasurable.

While this was happening, the Chief of the women's village found Old Man's tracks and sent a young woman to follow them and report what she had found. The young scout soon found the men's camp and watched from a hiding place for a while. She then hurried back, very excited to tell her news. "Oh, sisters, there is a camp with human beings in it. They are taller and stronger than we and have shooting sticks and much meat of different kinds. Surely they are never hungry and live very well." The women heard this and said, "If only they would come here and kill food for us!" Just then they saw the men coming over the hill. The women looked at the men and were frightened by these filthy creatures with matted hair and rawhide loincloths, unwashed and smelling foul. "We don't want people like these!" they said, and threw rocks at the men and shouted, "Go away!" As the men ran away, Old Man thought, "These creatures are dangerous. It was right that I put them far away." And the men returned to their own village.

Later the women talked together and the Chief said, "Maybe these dirty creatures don't know any better. We could teach them and make clothes for them. They might not be bad after all. They do look strong and are good hunters."

Back at the men's camp, Old Man decided that they should try again and told the men to wash themselves and make their hair in a handsome way and put on their best clothes. He led the men back to the women's camp, but when they arrived the women were butchering a kill of buffalo and were in their

Companions, 1995
Mixed media on paper, 30 x 40 in.

oldest garments, covered in blood, their hair matted and smelling terrible. The men were horrified by these creatures who looked so wild, and they went running back to their own camp. The women's Chief saw this and thought, "It seems we can't do anything right. Nothing we do is understood!" She gathered the women together and they decided to try one more time. They bathed in the river, combed their beautiful hair, put on their best doeskin garments and moccasins, and went again to the men's camp.

In the men's camp, Old Man was very cross. The men asked him what was the matter, and he said, "I wish the women were beautiful and sweet smelling and friendly." "We wish that, too," said the men. Just then a lookout came running. "The women are marching toward our camp. They probably want to kill us. Quickly get your bows and arrows!" "No, wait," said Old Man. "Instead, put on your best clothes and smoke yourselves with cedar and gather at the entrance to the village." Quickly, the men did as Old Man ordered. And when they had gathered they heard the soft singing of the women as they approached the village. They were resplendent in their brightly colored clothes and smelled of sweet grass. Old Man exclaimed, "How beautiful they are!

They delight my eyes and my nose and my ears!" "They make our hearts leap!" said the men.

The women's Chief said to her followers, "Why, these men are not so bad after all. The sound of their voices thrills my ears and the sight of their strong arms pleases my eyes!" Old Man went to the women's Chief and said, "Let us talk together." And they went to a quiet place alone. The woman Chief found Old Man pleasing and his heart pounded when he looked at her. "Let's try one thing we have never tried before," he said. "I like to try new things," she replied. "Maybe we should lie down to try this," he said. "Maybe that would be best," she replied. After a while Old Man said, "This is surely the most wonderful thing that ever happened to me." "And I," said the woman Chief. "I never dreamed anything could feel so good. It cannot be described. Let us go and tell the others!"

When they got back to camp, no one was there. All the men and women had paired off and found quiet spots of their own. They didn't need to be told about this wonderful new thing. They already knew.

And then there were children.

A tale of the BLOOD PIEGAN

The Warrior Maiden

LONG, LONG AGO, the Oneida people were beset by their old enemies the Mingoe, who had laid waste their villages, killed their men and boys, and abducted their women and children. Now there could be no resistance because the Mingoe were as numerous as grains of sand on the shore.

The Oneida took what was left of their tribe and hid in the deep forests on desolate mountains, where the Great Spirit gave them refuge from their enemies. Their supplies of food dwindled, and they could see that they would soon starve. The warrior chiefs and sachems met in council but could find no way to solve the problems that beset their people.

A young girl stepped forward and told the council of a dream that had showed her the way to save her people. Her name was Aliquipiso, and she was not afraid to give her life for the lives of those she loved, and so she told them the way of the dream. "The mountain on which we hide has at the top a sheer cliff. The men and boys will go and collect many heavy, sharp rocks and boulders and bring them to the edge of the cliff and wait and watch. I will go to the Mingoe and lead them to the place below this cliff, and as they stand at the bottom the men and boys will send the rocks and boulders down on them so that they will be destroyed."

With great wonder, the elders considered her dream and saw the wisdom of it. They honored her, saying, "The Great Spirit has blessed you, Aliquipiso, with courage and deep wisdom. We, your people, will always remember you."

The next morning Aliquipiso left the mountains to wander in the woods, pretending to be lost. The Mingoe found her, as she had hoped, and brought her to their warrior chief.

"Show us the way to where your people hide. If you do so we will adopt and care for you. If you refuse you will be tortured at the stake." Aliquipiso refused, and, as was their custom, they tied her to a tree stump and tortured her with fire, which she endured with great courage. At last she pretended to weaken and agreed to show them the way. That night the Mingoe bound her hands behind her and set her to walk in front of them, threatening to kill her if she betrayed them. All through the night she led them. Just before dawn, she gathered them below the towering cliff, saying, "Come close, Mingoe warriors, gather round me. The Oneida are sleeping and think they are safe. I will show you a way upward and you may surprise them." And so in the dawn's early light they crowded around Aliquipiso. It is then that Aliquipiso cried, "Oneida! The enemy are here! Destroy them!"

The Mingoe scarcely had time to strike her down before they themselves were rained upon by great boulders, which crushed and buried them. So many Mingoe warriors died that the remaining Mingoe returned to their own land and never made war on the Oneida again.

Aliquipiso's story has been told for many generations around Oneida campfires. The Great Spirit changed Aliquipiso's hair into woodbine, which the Oneida call "running hairs" and which is good medicine. From her body sprang sweet honeysuckle, which even today is known to her people as the "blood of brave women."

A tale of the ONEIDA

Touched by Mother Earth, 1994
Mixed media on paper, 50 x 40 in.

The Wolf Man

A YOUNG WOMAN lived with her parents. They wished for her to find a husband, but she did not want to marry.

One day, while taking a long walk, the young woman came upon a house she had never seen before. It stood all by itself and had a tall pole in front of it. She went in, but no one was there. There was much food, but the girl saw no woman's things. She stayed for a while and then heard someone coming. It was a handsome young man. He was wearing a fine squirrel parka that had a good wolf ruff. He looked like a wealthy young man.

The young man asked her if she had had something to eat. When she answered "no," he kindly invited her to eat with him. He told her he would be glad to have the company as he was always alone. After they ate, he asked her to stay with him, and she was happy to do so. Soon after that he asked her to be his wife.

The young man went out hunting every day. When he left in the morning, he would tell his wife, "Have something to eat. Don't do any hard work, just eat." Soon the young woman started to gain weight. Her husband seemed pleased that she was growing fatter every day.

One day the young woman was outside and looked up to see a raven perched on top of the pole in front of the house. From then on, the raven came and sat on top of the pole every day after the husband left to go hunting. One day the raven spoke to the young woman and said, "Be careful—one day your husband may decide to eat you, maybe tomorrow or one day soon. It would be wise for you to climb this pole tomorrow when he goes hunting."

Before dark the next day the woman climbed to the top of the pole and waited. Soon the husband came home and went into the house. Finding no one inside, he came out and looked all around, going right by the pole. He went back and forth looking for his wife and finally went into the house. A short time later a large, handsome wolf came out of the house, snarling and looking all around. The young woman was very frightened, but she kept still. Soon the wolf gave up searching and went off into the night. When the woman felt safe she climbed down the pole and ran as fast as she could back to her village. When she got home she asked her parents to find a good husband for her, and they soon did.

A tale of the INUIT

The Red Road Brings Us Home, 1994
Mixed media on paper, 60 x 40 in.

The Spirit-Wife

A YOUNG MAN was grieving the death of his beautiful wife. Sitting at her grave, he decided that he would follow her to the Land of the Dead. He made prayer sticks and sprinkled corn pollen and colored an eagle feather with red earth. Late in the night his wife's spirit appeared, smiling at him and saying, "Do not weep for me, for I am just leaving one life for another." "I love you too much to be without you," the young man said. "I ask to go with you to the Land of the Dead." His spirit-wife tried hard to talk him out of this idea, but at last she gave in, saying, "If you must, follow me, but I will be invisible to you in the daylight. Place the red eagle plume in my hair so that you will not lose sight of me."

The husband did as he was commanded. As the sun rose, his spirit-wife faded from sight, but the red plume did not disappear and he was able to follow her as she moved swiftly toward the Land of the Evening. Soon the husband tired and the plume was a long way ahead of him. He called out, "Beloved wife, wait for me. I can't run any longer." The plume stopped, but when he caught up it continued. After several days, the young husband grew so weary he could barely walk, though each night the spirit-wife would appear, encouraging him to continue.

One day the plume led him to a great precipice and just floated across the chasm. The husband called, "Dear wife, wait for me." But he didn't know how he would cross this steep canyon. As he pondered a tiny striped squirrel came to him, saying, "Do not despair, I will help you." The creature took a tiny seed from its mouth pouch and put it in a crevice on the canyon wall. It moistened this with its saliva and then sang,

"*Tsithl, tsithl, tsithl*, tall stalk, tall stalk, tall stalk." Out of the rock sprouted a long stalk that quickly spanned the chasm. The young man crossed over to find the plume awaiting him. He again followed the plume that danced so swiftly.

That evening they arrived at a large, dark lake, and the plume plunged into the center of the lake. He called to his spirit-wife, for he could not follow. He waited, but she did not appear. He lay down and wept. Then he heard someone calling, "Hu-hu-hu," and he felt soft wings fluttering on his back. He looked up and saw an owl hovering above him. The owl asked him why he wept, and he said, "My beloved wife is deep in the lake, in the Land of the Dead, and I cannot follow." The owl said, "I will help you. Follow me to my house in the mountains." He followed the owl to a cave high in the mountains. Once inside, he saw many other owl men and women. They greeted him warmly and bade him rest and gave him food and drink. After he had rested and eaten, the owl man who had brought him there took a medicine bundle from the wall, saying, "You must listen very carefully to my instructions and be patient and curb your youthful desires, or this medicine will be of no help." The husband promised, and the owl continued. "This is sleep medicine. You will fall into a deep sleep and be transported to another place. When you awake, you will find your spirit-wife. As the sun rises she will smile at you in the flesh and she will be spirit no more, and so you will live happily. You must remember to curb your eagerness. Let not your desire to embrace her get the better of you, for if you touch her before bringing her to the village of your birth, she will be lost to you forever." Saying this, the

Beautiful Spirit-Wife (detail), 1995
Mixed media on paper, 33½ x 22 in.

owl blew the sleep medicine into the young husband's eyes and he fell into a deep slumber.

The owl beings flew the husband to the lake, laid him on the shore, and descended to the bottom of the lake, the Land of the Dead. They put the guardian spirits to sleep, lay a tribute of prayer sticks on the altar of the netherworld, and took the spirit-wife and flew her to the surface, laying her gently next to her husband.

When the husband awoke, he found his beloved wife beside him, still asleep in the light of the morning sun. He was filled with happiness, but he remembered the owl's warning and did not touch his wife. She awoke smiling at him, saying, "Truly, your love for me is stronger than even death."

They began the journey back to the village of their birth. The husband was careful to follow the owl's instructions and did not embrace or touch his beloved wife. In the middle of the fourth day, the sun was very hot and the wife asked to rest in the shade. As they were not far from the village, they lay down and she soon slept. Her husband lay beside her, gazing on her beautiful face. Without thinking, he reached out and gently touched the cheek he loved so much. She awoke instantly and, weeping, said, "You loved me greatly, but your desire overcame your restraint, and now I must die again." And she faded from sight. On a branch above, an owl hooted mournfully, and the husband's eyes appeared empty, as though he had lost his own soul as well.

If only the young husband had waited a short time, death would have been overcome. But if there were no death, the earth would soon be too crowded and all the people would then live in misery. So it may be that what happened is for the best.

A tale of the ZUNI

The Old Woman Who Lives in the Moon

OLD WOMAN Who Never Dies lives in the Moon. She has three sons. The oldest is called Day, the middle is called Sun, and the youngest is Night. She also has three daughters. The oldest is called Morning Star: Woman Who Carries a Feather. The second is Striped Pumpkin: She Who Circles Around the Pole Star. And the youngest is called Evening Star.

Old Woman Who Never Dies is a great help to the people, for it is she who sends messengers in the form of wild birds to signal the proper times to plant and harvest. In the spring she sends wild geese to say it is time to plant corn. When the swans come it is time to plant pumpkins, and when the ducks come the beans will grow well.

When the birds appear it is time for the people to celebrate the Corn Festival. They build a special scaffold to hold up the dry meat. The old women bring a staff tied with an ear of corn, and they dance around this place while the old men drum for them and rattle hollow pumpkins filled with seeds. This is to honor Old Woman Who Never Dies.

In the fall the people again put out dried meat for Old Woman Who Never Dies, and they pray to her to send buffalo and deer, so that the people will not starve over the winter. Old Woman Who Never Dies is fond of dried meat. The birds help pick the dried meat from the scaffolds, and then they fly back to Old Woman Who Never Dies and live with her for the winter.

In the old days, it is said, Old Woman Who Never Dies lived near the Small Missouri River, and that the people could visit her. She always had a small kettle of cooked corn, and no matter how many visitors were there it was never empty, for it could fill itself over and over. Old Woman Who Never Dies watches over the cornfield with the help of the white-tailed deer, the blackbirds, and the many mice and moles, so that the fields will be ready for planting in the spring.

A tale of the MANDAN

She Lives Within the Moonlight (detail), 1995
Mixed media on paper, 50 x 30 in.

The Origin of Corn

A LONG TIME AGO, when Indians were first made, there lived one alone, far, far from any others. He knew not fire, and he subsisted on roots and bark and nuts. This Indian became very lonesome for company. He grew tired of digging roots and lost his appetite, and for several days he lay dreaming in the sunshine; when he awoke he saw something standing near. At first he was very frightened of it. But when it spoke, his heart was glad, for it was a beautiful woman with long, light hair, very unlike any Indian. He asked her to come to him, but she would not. If he tried to approach her, she seemed to go farther away. He sang to her of his loneliness and beseeched her not to leave him. At last she told him that if he would do just as she said, he would always have her with him. He promised that he would.

Leading him to where there was some very dry grass, the light-haired woman told the man to get two very dry sticks and rub them together quickly, holding them in the grass. Soon a spark flew out; the grass caught it, and quick as an arrow the ground was burned over. Then she said, "When the sun sets, take me by the hair and drag me over the burned ground." He did not want to do this. But she told him that wherever he dragged her, something like grass would spring up, and he would see her hair coming from between the leaves; then the seeds would be ready for his use. He did as she said, and to this day, when they see the silk hair on the cornstalk, the people know she has not forgotten.

A tale of the ABANAKI

Her Beauty Comes from Mother Earth, 1995
Mixed media on canvas, 36 x 36 in.

The Seven Stars of the Big Dipper

AT NIGHT in the northern sky, we can see seven stars. They were once children. Long ago there was a family with eight children, six boys and two girls. The oldest girl had many suitors, but she refused to marry any of them. Every day she went into the forest to gather wood for cooking. One day her younger sister followed her, and to her surprise, when they entered the forest the elder sister disappeared. After a long while she reappeared, her robes covered with earth and leaves. The younger sister thought, "I must find out what my sister does when she goes to the forest alone." For many days she secretly followed her sister into the forest, and the elder sister always disappeared. The younger sister was about to give up on this mystery when she saw her sister playing with a large bear. Then she understood why her sister refused to marry any of the boys of the village. She ran back and told her father what she had seen. The father called his five older sons and said to them, "I have a bear as a son-in-law, and he lives in the forest. This is very bad. We must kill this bear." And so they did.

The girl stood by the corpse of her lover, the bear, and wept and wept. His spirit came to her in a dream and gave her his powers. He told her to take a piece of his hide as an amulet, for it would do many miraculous things. She did as he said and found that indeed this amulet had magical powers.

One day when her five older brothers were out hunting, the elder sister turned herself into a bear and killed all the people in the camp except her sister and her younger brother. From then on, these three lived together and the younger sister served the elder sister.

While at the river getting water one day, the younger sister saw her five brothers returning. She told them the story of their older sister's revenge and said that they must not return or they, too, would be killed. The five brothers tried to figure out how they could save their younger brother and sister from the Bear Woman. Soon they had a plan. They picked prickly pears, and when it was dark they scattered them all around the lodge of the Bear Woman, leaving a small patch clear. In the night one of the brothers crept into the lodge and carried the children away. When Bear Woman awoke, she saw that the children were gone. She turned herself into a bear and began to follow them, but the thorns from the prickly pears got into her feet and she had to stop and pull them out. This gave the others time to flee deeper into the forest.

One of the five brothers, Little Eagle, was a medicine man. He had a bow with magical arrows and a magical feather that he wore in his hair. Each time he heard the bear sister approaching, he used the feather to keep her away. First he put a large lake between them, then a great thicket; but the Bear Woman always followed. The third time, he conjured up a large tree, and all the brothers and the younger sister climbed into the high branches. When Bear Woman saw this she said, "Now you cannot escape. I will kill you all." And she began to climb the tree. Little Eagle shot many of his magical arrows, but they did not kill Bear Woman. A little bird appeared saying, "Aim at the parting of her hair. You must hit the Bear Woman between the eyes."

Bear's Path Is Introspection, 1994
Mixed media on canvas, 50 x 70 in.

Bear Woman was coming after Little Eagle when he took aim with his arrow and shot her between the eyes. She fell dead at the bottom of the tree. All the brothers and the younger sister climbed down from the tree and looked at their older sister, who was dead and no longer had the form of a bear. They all felt sad for her and for everyone who had died because of her love for a bear.

Then Little Eagle said, "What shall we do? Our relatives and friends are all dead, and we have no place to go." The oldest brother said, "Let's go to heaven. We will become the stars in the northern sky. Then all the people will know that we are the ones who send the morning."

Little Eagle took his feather and waved it over his head. The brothers took the same positions as in the tree. Little Eagle took his position with his younger sister, now a small star, at his side.

And so these stars came into being. Every night you can see them walk across the sky until they disappear in the morning light.

A tale of the BLACKFOOT

Brave Woman Counts Coup

THERE WAS A GREAT CHIEF who in his youth had been a mighty warrior. He had three sons and one daughter. The sons tried to be as brave and mighty as their father. They went out to fight the Crow, their enemies, with reckless bravery, always in the front rank. One by one they were killed, leaving only the daughter, who was called Winyan Okitika, which means Brave Woman. Many young men had asked for Brave Woman's hand, and she was much loved by two young men— Red Horn, a chief's son, and Little Eagle, a poor boy. But she refused all suitors, saying, "I will not take a husband until I have avenged the deaths of my brothers."

At that time the Crow nation wished to take the land on the banks of the Missouri, which the Sioux considered their own. The Sioux decided to send a war party, and Brave Woman begged her father to let her go. Finally, in sorrow, he agreed. She put on her best dress of white buckskin and took a fine horse, and her father gave her his war club. Both Red Horn and Little Eagle joined the war party. Brave Woman gave them her dead brothers' weapons, saying, "Count coup for my brothers, whose weapons these are." She herself would carry only the war club. And so they rode to battle.

At first Brave Woman stayed back and supported the warriors by singing brave-heart songs and making the trilling sound with which Sioux women support their men. But the battle was going badly and her group was driven back by the overwhelming numbers of Crow. Using her war club, she rode into battle. She did not try to kill the enemy warriors, but, using the club, she touched them left and right, counting coup for her dead brothers. The Sioux warriors, seeing her bravery, could not retreat and so surged forward with great energy. It was a terrible battle. Brave Woman's horse went down and she was on foot and defenseless. Red Horn passed on his speckled pony, but she was too proud to call to him for help and he pretended not to see her. Then Little Eagle saw her and came riding to her. He dismounted, giving her his pony. She mounted, expecting that he would ride behind her, but he said the horse was wounded and too weak to carry both of them. "I won't leave you to be killed," she said, but Little Eagle hit the horse sharply with her dead brother's bow and it bolted as Little Eagle went into the battle on foot.

Brave Woman rallied the warriors for a final charge, her bravery calling forth such fury from the warriors that they drove the enemy from the land for good. It was a great victory, but many men died. One of these was Little Eagle. For his bravery he was honored by the tribe. Brave Woman mourned Little Eagle, saying that she was his widow, although in life he had never dared speak to her. She gashed her arms and tore her buckskin dress in mourning. She never took a husband and never ceased to mourn Little Eagle. She died of old age, greatly honored, and her fame endures.

A tale of the WHITE RIVER SIOUX

Great Chief's Daughter, 1995
Mixed media on canvas, 50 x 40 in.

How Men Came to Dominate Women

ONE DAY, while out collecting firewood, the women of the Mundurucu heard strange and compelling music. They followed the sounds and came to a beautiful lake that no one had ever seen. The music seemed to come from the dark depths of the still water. The women knew they must find the source of this music, which made them feel strong and happy. They gathered vines and made a net to pull through the waters. Soon they caught three fishes, which immediately turned into three flutes. The women went home playing these magical instruments, which they found gave them power over the men.

They spent their days playing music, and now the men had to collect firewood, bring water, and make manioc cakes. (To this day men's hands are flat from many years of making manioc cakes.) The men also had to hunt, for the flutes required offerings of meat to satisfy the souls of the ancestors who lived in the powerful instruments.

After much time, the men grew angry at all the work they had to do, and they refused to hunt unless the women handed over the flutes. As it was forbidden for women to hunt, and they did not wish to anger the souls of the ancestors, they gave the flutes to the men. From that time on, men had power over women. The flutes could not be looked upon by any woman. Women had to close themselves in their huts when the flutes were played. Soon there were no women who remembered that they had once played the flutes and had power over men. It is only ignorance that keeps women from regaining their power.

A tale of the MUNDURUCU

Halfsides, 1994
Mixed media on paper, 45 x 50 in.

The Foolish Girls

LONG AGO, some people were camping in birch bark lodges. With them were two very foolish girls who always slept outside the lodge, in the open. Self-respecting girls didn't do this, only foolish, man-hungry ones. So there they were, looking at the sky, giggling.

One of the girls said to the other, "Look at those stars, the white one and the red one."

"I'd like to sleep with a star. They must be good lovers, really hot ones," said the other.

"Me, too. I want a star under the blanket with me," said her friend. "I'll take the red star to bed, and you can have the white one."

"All right," said her companion, and they drifted off to sleep.

When they awoke they found themselves in the upper world, and the red and white stars were men who said to the girls, "You desire to sleep with us, and here we are. Let's do it!" So they did. The girl who had chosen the red star found that he was a vigorous young man and kept her busy all night long. She liked this very much. But the other girl's star man was an old white star, and he could no longer perform very well. She asked her friend to swap husbands for a while, but her friend did not want to do so.

For a while they lived with their star husbands, but then they became dissatisfied and missed their lives on Earth. The girl with the young star felt tired; she complained to her friend that her lover wore her out. "It's too much," she said. "I can't stand doing it all the time." The other girl was bored and said, "This star lover of mine is too old to do anything at all."

They had found out that star lovers are just like any other lovers. They wanted to go home as it was now winter and they missed playing in the snow with the other young people, and they wanted new young Ojibway men to sleep with.

One day they saw an old woman sitting on a hole in the sky. When she moved the girls could see the Earth down below. They saw their village and became sad. They asked the old woman how they could get down to the village, and she gave them plants and taught them to make rope out of the fibers in the plants. The girls set about making rope, which was a tedious job. Soon they grew bored with this job, for they were not only foolish and fickle but also lazy. They asked their star husbands to help them by holding the ropes so that they could go and visit their families on Earth. (They were also liars. They did not intend to return.)

The girls started climbing down the ropes, but the ropes were too short; they landed at the top of a very tall pine tree, in

Star Sisters, 1995
Mixed media on paper, 35 x 44¾ in.

an old eagles' nest, and they couldn't figure out a way to get down. Just then a bear came lumbering by, and they called to him, "Hey, Bear, I bet you'd like some good-looking girls to sleep with. Help us get down on the ground and we will sleep with you." The bear was wise, and he saw that the girls were foolish, and forward as well. He told them he couldn't climb so high and went away, not even looking back.

Next a buffalo passed under the tree. The girls called out to him, "Oh, powerful one, help us down from this tree and you can sleep with us." The buffalo saw that they were pretty, and he tried and tried to climb the tree. Soon he got tired and didn't care if he got to sleep with these girls. He went away saying, "Hooves are no good for climbing trees. Find somebody with claws!"

Old man coyote came by, but he said he had a jealous wife and couldn't help the girls or he would get a bad beating.

So there they were, and it was getting dark and cold. Then they saw a wolverine, who was so ugly no girls would sleep with him. Surely he would try hard to help them get down. "Hey, handsome, get us out of this tree and we will sleep with you." In a wink of an eye, the wolverine was up the tree. He carried the first girl down and greedily enjoyed himself with her. He did the same with the second girl. He was rough and the girls did not enjoy this one bit. This went on into the night, but when the wolverine fell asleep the girls were able to sneak away. As they walked to their village, one girl said to the other, "I think we have done some stupid things. When we finally get back to our village, I shall be very content. And I will never again sleep outside the lodge." The other girl agreed completely.

A tale of the OJIBWAY

The Girl Who Helped Thunder

LONG AGO among the Muskogee people there lived a girl who had mastered the bow and arrow and was a skilled hunter. She looked forward to the day she would be asked to join her people's hunting party. Finally that day came, and her uncle asked her to go to the mountains with her male relatives. When she got to the camp she realized that she was there to cook and take care of the camp. She didn't complain, though, and she did her best to complete her duties.

One day while she was cooking, she heard the rumble of thunder. It seemed to be coming from a stream close by and not from the sky. She rushed to the water and found an old man struggling to get away from a snake. Each time the man thrashed, thunder rolled. The snake and the man both called for the girl to help. The man cried, "Shoot the white spot on the snake's neck or he will drown me." The snake cried, "Shoot the man or his thunder will kill you." The girl remembered that thunder brings rain, which helps the corn grow, and she raised her bow and killed the snake. The old man was Thunder, and he told the girl that he would always be her friend. He told her that her people would have trouble and what she could do to help them. He told her to purify and to do the medicine fast for spiritual guidance. He taught her a song that would give her great power, saying that she was to use it only if her people were in great danger.

After returning to the village and asking repeatedly, the girl convinced her uncle to make arrangements for her purification ceremony and medicine fast. During her fast the words of Thunder came back to her: "I will give you the power to help."

In the fall of the same year while most men were away hunting, a great party of Cherokee warriors approached the village. The uncle, remembering that she was a skilled hunter, went to get the girl to help fight the enemy with him. He saw her walking away from the village, going toward the east. She walked around the village in a great circle four times, singing in a language he had never heard. She then took the shape of a rainbow. From high above she lifted her bow and began firing white-hot bolts of lightning. Thunder rolled as her arrows exploded at the feet of the enemy. She returned to her own shape when the enemy warriors were all dead or captured. She told the captives to return to their people and tell them what had happened, and to never return.

To this day the story is told of how The Girl Who Helped Thunder used the sacred power given to her to save her people.

A tale of the MUSKOGEE

Her Open Heart Reveals Her Wisdom, 1994
Mixed media on canvas, 64 x 60 in.

Emerging into the Upper World

IN THE BEGINNING, two sisters were born underground. There was no light, but they knew each other through the sense of touch. As they grew, the spirit Tsitctinako told them to be patient and wait until the time when they would emerge from the darkness of the underground into the light.

One day they found baskets that contained seeds and little images of animals. They planted some of the seeds. The plants that grew from them pushed up through the earth, with the help of some of the animals the sisters had brought to life from the little images.

Then Tsitctinako said to the sisters, "It is time for you to go out." He instructed them to wait for the sun to rise in the direction called the east, and to thank it for bringing them light. Tsitctinako said that to their right side would be the direction called the south; behind them would be the west, where the sun would set daily; and to their left would be the north.

The sisters, Ia'tik and Nao'tsiti, were instructed to bring everything in their baskets to life as they had been created to help the Great Spirit complete the world. They planted all their seeds, praying every morning to the sun and offering pollen and cornmeal as they had been shown by Tsitctinako. They brought all the animals in their baskets to life, one by one, telling each its name with its first breath. The sisters formed the mountains by throwing stones from their baskets in the four directions. Then they told each animal where it should live and what it should eat.

One day Nao'tsiti encountered a snake, who told her she could bear a child in her likeness by going to the rainbow and receiving its drops of water into her body. She did this and gave birth to two sons. But the sisters had been told by Tsitctinako to be patient about having children. Since Nao'tsiti did not wait as she had been told, Tsitctinako left them alone in the world.

Ia'tik sought her own place, taking one of Nao'tsiti's sons with her. The sisters were now separated for life. Ia'tik bore many children with Nao'tsiti's son. As her children increased in number, she created the spirit of winter to live in the north, the spirit of spring to live in the west, the spirit of summer to live in the south, and the spirit of autumn to live in the east. She taught winter to bring snow, spring to warm the world, and summer to heat it. Autumn, disliking the smell of plants and fruits, was taught to destroy them. Ia'tik taught her children to pray to these spirits for moisture, warmth, ripening, and frost. Ia'tik then created many gods from the dirt left in her basket. She gave each one a costume and a prayer and then created a god to rule over all of them. And everything was as it should be.

A tale of the ACOMA

The Sisters, 1994
Mixed media on paper, 40 x 50 in.

The Wolves and the Caribou Woman

LONG AGO in Alaska there was a woman who lived all alone with no parents, husband, or children. She had a difficult time getting enough food. All during the summer months she had barely enough food to stay alive. When winter came she had nothing at all to eat in her igloo. One cold day she went out to a little stream near Hooper Bay. With a bone ice chisel she cut a hole in the ice, piling the cakes beside her sled, on which she carried her fishing gear. She spread her old grass mat as a windbreak, as all Eskimo people do when they are fishing, and put her old tom cod net into the water.

As she waited for a tom cod, she looked out over the tundra and saw a dark shape moving quickly toward her. Soon she could see it was a caribou running hard. It came right up to the woman, looking quite frightened. The woman was astonished that the animal would come so close to her. Suddenly the caribou reached up with a forefoot and pulled back the skin of its face. Inside was a woman! "Oh, please help me!" she cried. "There are wolves after me, and I can run no farther. Help me escape my death!"

"I will hide you, poor thing," said the Eskimo woman. "Jump in here." And she made a hiding place in the center of the ice cakes. The caribou jumped in and the woman covered her with the straw mat, as she heard the howling approach of the wolves. Soon they were upon her. The leader of the wolves did a strange thing. He reached up and with his front paw pulled back the skin of his face. He was a man! "Tell me," he said, "have you seen the caribou my brothers and I have been chasing?" "Yes," replied the woman, "I saw a caribou running like the wind. She went

past here toward the mountains yonder. She must be very far away by now."

The leader of the wolves quickly put his wolf face back in place. He walked right past the blocks of ice where the caribou was hiding. The old woman shook with fright because she feared that the wolf might scent the animal covered with the grass mat. But he did not. Away the wolves went in full cry as fast as they could. The old woman went on with her fishing, and the caribou woman remained hidden. This was fortunate, for before long, from far across the tundra the woman heard a wolf singing. She could see it was an old wolf, for he did not move as swiftly as the others. Soon she could hear the words of his song:

I am old and can run no more,
My teeth are worn, my paws are sore,
I'll follow my sons over the hill
And eat the caribou they kill.
Aw-oo-oo-oo, Aw-oo-oo-oo.

The old woman trembled with fear, as did the caribou woman hiding under the mat. But the old wolf went on, singing:

The caribou's heart is very sweet.
That is the first thing I'll eat,
I'll have steaks and ribs to eat my fill
When I reach my sons just over the hill.
Aw-oo-oo-oo. Aw-oo-oo-oo.

Wolf Cry, 1995
Mixed media on canvas, 50 x 70 in.

When he was out of sight, the old woman uncovered the caribou. "Mercy," she said, "those wolves make me shiver. My dear friend, you had better run quickly back the way you came, before they return. Run in your old tracks, then they will never know which way you went." The caribou woman stood and shook herself. She said, "I do not know how to thank you for saving my life, but maybe I can help you." She knelt down on the ice and seemed to pull her shiny hooves right inside her legs, as though they were sleeves. She pulled out a great pile of caribou fat and gave it to the old woman. "Here is some delicious fat for you," she said, "and may you always have good luck with your fishing and plenty to eat." And with that the caribou woman trotted away.

The old woman was so happy to get this great boon of sweet caribou fat that she burst into tears. (Eskimo people need much fat to keep their bodies warm in such a cold climate.) Then she looked to her fishing net and found it so heavy that she could barely lift it. It was filled with a great tom cod. Soon she had so many cod that she filled her whole sled. This food would last a long time, and she was very happy indeed.

From then on the old woman always caught all the fish she needed. In the summer she found lots of greens and berries. Eskimo people say that she had such good luck because she had been so kind to the caribou woman, who made good medicine for the poor woman so that she would never again go hungry.

A tale of the INUIT

The Girl Who Was Loved by Dogs

THERE ONCE was a little girl who lived in a very old and beautiful city by a bay. Her favorite place to play and spend her days was in the park that was directly across from her house. This park was filled with every variety of flower, which alternated blooming during the winter, spring, summer, and fall—carnations, roses, poppies, and pansies; red, pink, white, and yellow; speckled, spotted, glowing, and growing.

It was always a thrill for this little girl to put on her pink coat with its matching pink hat and travel across the street with her parents to the park. These days spent at the park, however, always ended in tears for the little girl when it was time to leave. Her parents didn't understand the source of her tears, but the little girl knew what made her cry. She was lonely when she wasn't in the park. She didn't have brothers or sisters but was known as an Only Child because she was the only child her parents had.

At the park the little girl saw lots of people with their dogs, and none of these people seemed to be lonely. She thought, "Yes, a dog will be my companion—a dog to live with me, eat and sleep with me, dance and sing and play with me. It will be like having my best friend stay with me all the time."

The very first dog that she got, she won on a children's television program by sending in a postcard and having it drawn out of a twirling drum. The dog was a black cocker spaniel and she named him Stuffy. She was six years old, and Stuffy was a puppy. He danced, he sang (in dog language, of course), he played with the little girl and made her very happy. This dog would be the first of many dogs she would have while growing from a girl to a woman. Her other dogs were Blondie, Thumper, Twigga, Wrinkles, Tarzan, Nancy, Pants, Phantom, Shadow, and Dexter. They were basset hound, German shepherd, Labrador retriever, and many others of unknown parentage. Some were tall, some were short, some had short hair, some had long hair, but all of them were like having her best friend spend the night forever. She always had the right house and yard to have a dog companion, and so she was never without dog love, and never lonely.

The ancient people say that the Great Creator made all the animals on one side of a very steep cliff and all the humans on the other side of this cliff, and that before he completed the humans the dogs jumped across this divide to be with the humans. And they say this is how dog became man's best friend. This woman is sure this story is true.

A tale of Patricia Wyatt

My Dog Companions, 1995
Mixed media on paper, 40 x 32 in.